SIX STEPS FORWARD

AUTHOR VOICE

Six Steps FORWARD

A Simple, Practical Guide to Managing Cashflow, Building Wealth, and Leaving a Legacy

DAVID R. PETERS

CPA, CFP®, CLU, CPCU

Six Steps Forward: A Simple, Practical Guide to Managing Cashflow, Building Wealth, and Leaving a Legacy

Library of Congress Control Number: xxxxxxxxxx
ISBN: 978-1-969935-39-8 (paperback) 978-1-969935-40-4 (ebook)

Editors: Abigail Dengler, Jennifer Casey
Cover and Interior Design: Emma Elzinga

Printed in the United States of America

First Edition

3 West Garden Street, Ste. 718
Pensacola, FL 32502

Published by Author Voice Publishing
An Imprint of Indigo River Publishing
www.authorvoicepublishing.com

Ordering Information:

Quantity sales: Special discounts are available on quantity purchases by corporations, associations, and others. For details, contact the publisher at the address above.

Orders by US trade bookstores and wholesalers: Please contact the publisher at the address above.

With Indigo River Publishing, you can always expect great books, strong voices, and meaningful messages. Most importantly, you'll always find . . . *words worth reading.*

The content presented in this book is for informational purposes only, is general in nature, and is not intended to and should not be relied upon or construed as financial, investment, or estate planning advice. This does not constitute an offer to sell or a solicitation to buy any security, investment, or planning product. Past performance is not indicative of future results. All investments involve risk, including the possible loss of principal. Please consult with a financial advisor to assess your individual situation.

Financial and investment advisory services offered through Peters Financial LLC. David Peters also offers tax services through Peters Tax Preparation & Consulting, PC, and insurance services through David Peters Insurance Agency LLC. Peters Tax Preparation & Consulting, PC, and David Peters Insurance Agency LLC are affiliated with Peters Financial LLC through common ownership. Clients or prospective clients are never obligated to use Peters Tax Preparation & Consulting, PC, or David Peters Insurance Agency LLC as part of any financial planning or investment management services offered by Peters Financial LLC.

To my parents,
who believed in me and
always pushed me to follow my dreams.

Contents

Introduction

"Why do they always make things so complicated?"

My client didn't even look up as he said these words. He was sitting in a green leather chair in our waiting area, eyeing the television in the corner. A 24/7 news channel was on, displaying the constant stock ticker at the bottom of the screen. I'd worked in that office for six months, and I barely noticed we even had a TV anymore. It was all white noise at this point.

"Excuse me?" I asked him, perplexed.

He shook his head.

"That last story," he said. "Build your financial future. It is important to save. It is important to think ahead. No one argues with that stuff. But then they proceed to tell me a bunch of gibberish that I can't use. Shouldn't this be simple? Why do they always make things so complicated? They all say they are making it simple, but then they say things no one can understand. Why is it this hard?"

"Well, it is only a seven-minute TV segment." I smiled wryly at my own wit. But I quickly realized he wasn't his normal jovial self on this one.

"No, I'm serious," he replied. "If someone were to give me a roadmap about how to achieve financial success, I would take it. You know. Like a recipe. I can follow a recipe. But this? This is just words for the sake of words."

I have worked in various parts of financial services for over twenty years. While this interaction with my client was only one instance, I have had this scenario play out many times in my office. Clients feel confused and overwhelmed by the abundance of financial tips and information they read about on the internet and see on TV. They feel like financial topics are over their head—and they want something easier.

This is why I have always believed my most important role was to be an educator. Whenever I prepared a tax return for a client, my goal was never just to get the deductions and income correct. It was to help the client see why they received the refund they did—and how this could be different next year. When I worked as a financial advisor, I wanted the clients to see the tradeoff between risk and return on a portfolio. I wanted them to see not only what investments they could choose, but why to choose one over another—and how each could contribute to their financial goals. Even in the world of insurance, I never wanted to just sell policies. I wanted clients to understand how those policies could serve them.

I have always looked at myself as being more of a guide than a guru—an educator more than someone who just executes. My goal has never been to just tell people what to do with their money. My goal has always been to take something seemingly out of reach and make it obtainable, understandable, and doable.

If you've ever felt like my client—eager to build your financial future but lacking direction—this book is for you. It's true that everyone's financial situation is different. It's true that everyone's financial goals are different. It is even true that future investment performance is never guaranteed. However, that doesn't mean there is no structure to building a financial plan. There is—and that's what this book is about.

It's a step-by-step guide on how to build a financial future for yourself and prioritize your financial goals.

Common Misconceptions About Financial Planning

Many financial advisors agree that you should prioritize certain financial goals over others. Trying to take care of everything all at once is usually too much for most people's brains to handle. It also generally leads to frustration; it's harder to see progress if you are trying to do too many things at once.

Most practitioners believe building an emergency fund should be the first priority in any financial plan. Of course, other goals like gifts and inheritance for grandchildren are important to save up for. But if a pipe is leaking, a plumber needs to be called today! Similarly, expenses like auto repairs or the family dog's medicine can't wait. Many times, the standard order of priorities makes sense.

However, the prioritization many financial advisors recommend is often difficult to implement for clients, because it ignores clients' practical concerns and can lead to many misconceptions and inadvertent mistakes. Clients tend to focus so heavily on certain areas of their financial lives that they ignore other parts. Let's examine a few of these.

Misconception #1: "I need to be debt-free before I can begin foundational financial tasks, including building an emergency fund."

Debt is a burden. It causes us to lose sleep at night and weighs on our brains. We worry about making the payments we need to afford our lifestyles, send our kids to college, and receive necessary medical treatment. However, focusing *only* on debt may actually hurt us in the long run.

Let's say you receive a $1,000 work bonus. You can use that bonus to take another $1,000 off your mortgage (which has a 4 percent interest rate), or you can invest the money in a savings account that earns 5 percent. If you pay down your mortgage, you save about $40 in interest ($1,000 x 4% = $40). But if you invest in your savings account, you will earn $50 ($1,000 x 5% = $50). With that $50, you could pay the additional interest on your mortgage and still have $10 left over.[1]

What's the point? Interest rates on debt may be higher or lower than what you could earn in a savings account or just in the markets in general. If you try to get rid of all your debt before you start saving or investing any of it, you may actually cost yourself an opportunity to make more money in the market.

Consider another potential missed opportunity: When you start working, many employers offer retirement accounts. Normally, an employer will put more money into a retirement plan on your behalf if *you* put in more money. This is referred to as an employer contribution or a match. You should normally try to contribute at least 10 to 15 percent of your paycheck to take advantage of employer matches. You will miss out on this contribution by trying to pay down all your debt before saving anything. Even if you are trying to pay your mortgage off quickly, it will normally take several years. These years are precious. Missing several years of potential retirement contributions could take you off track for your retirement savings. Plus, in general, the sooner you start saving for the future, the more money you will have in retirement due to compound interest and investment earnings. (More on this later.)

---

1 This example ignores compounding. However, compounding does not matter for purposes of illustrating the point—interest rates matter and it is not always best to pay down debt!

Misconception #2: "Taxes have no place in financial planning."

I have heard many financial advisors say they don't advise in any area of taxation. Financial advisors often have areas of expertise or specialization, and it would be the rarest of rare to find an advisor who is truly an expert in everything. (Not to mention, it's unethical for any financial advisor to advise you in an area they are not competent in.) Utilizing a specialized advisor in itself is not a problem and can be helpful. If you have complex needs, you may need someone who has deep knowledge of a particular area.

However, this can become problematic when clients mistakenly assume taxes should not be considered in a financial plan because many financial advisors do not practice in this area. This is a mistake. Every client, regardless of background or net worth, must deal with taxes. When you are working, tax planning strategies can allow you to take home a greater share of your paycheck. When you are in retirement, tax strategies can help you pull from retirement accounts more efficiently and ensure you don't inadvertently jump a tax bracket. When you are late in retirement, tax planning strategies can help you pass on wealth to younger generations and allow them to keep a greater portion. For these reasons, tax planning should have a place in *all* stages of a financial plan. It's often said that taxes are one of life's few certainties; if that's the case, they should definitely play a role in our financial planning!

Misconception #3: "Financial planning is for rich people."

Nothing could be further from the truth. Everyone deals with money and should have a plan for how to take care of it. It's true that many financial advisors have an account minimum, meaning a financial advisor may only accept you as a client if you have a certain net worth or dollars to invest. The more money you invest with them, the more they get paid, so account minimums ensure financial planners will make at least enough to cover their time and expenses. However, not *every* financial advisor requires a minimum (I have never had minimums in my own practice). Many have other strategies to ensure their own needs are covered.

I'm a firm believer that nearly anyone can benefit from financial planning. For some, financial planning may help them control their spending, start a budget, and cover their bills more easily. For others, financial advising may show them what retirement could be—and allow them to live better than they expected. For still others, financial planning may simply alleviate some of the anxiety that they have about their own money. In all of these cases, financial planning can lead to a deeper understanding of why someone's financial world is the way it is—and what they can do for it to be better.

In this book, we cover a variety of topics. Some, you can implement immediately. Others, you may not be ready for quite yet. My goal is to give you a path for financial planning success that will set you on the right path forward.

How Do I Build a Financial Plan for My Life?

There is a systematic way to achieve your financial goals. The purpose of this book is to provide a roadmap to building a financial plan and achieving your financial goals in a way that's easily implemented. In other words, this book is not a deep dive into investing or about financial planning theory. It's meant to provide practical, straightforward steps that most people can follow. It's also meant to change how you think about money so that you can take control of your own financial life—rather than feeling victimized by it. I'll also help you prioritize your goals so that you can see *real* progress and know where to focus. With these in mind, here are six steps to building your financial future:

1. Manage cash flow.
2. Protect your assets.
3. Invest in yourself and your career.
4. Invest in markets.
5. Take control of your tax return.
6. Prepare for retirement and leave a legacy.

In the following chapters, I'll show you why each step is important and how it contributes to your financial future—and provide plenty of ideas to chew on along the way.

Whenever I talk to clients about the six steps I have outlined in this book, their feedback is often one of disbelief. They always believe there should be something more to it. There should be some point where I tell them a complicated formula that will magically help them achieve their financial goals. But building your financial future does not need to be complicated or difficult. It *does* involve discipline. You need to be disciplined enough to follow the steps—and to start the steps over if something unexpected happens in your life.

We should be clear. Even if you follow these steps, you may still need to get an expert involved, like a financial advisor, tax accountant, insurance agent, or estate attorney. Why? Because everyone's situation is different. Different people need to invest in different things. Different people need different insurance policies. Different people are able to implement different tax strategies. However, we can lay out a roadmap of what to address and prioritize first for most people. Once you get to a step that you need help with, reach out to an expert. That' what they are there for!

Do the steps guarantee you will have millions of dollars and live a mansion? Of course not! However, if you focus on the steps, your uation can improve, and you can see your (reasonable) financial g become reality.

STEP 1

Manage Cash Flow

I sat there staring at the couple I'd been talking to for the last hour. I had just finished making some observations about their budget. I believe Bill was expecting me to scold his wife about her spending. He looked back at me, waiting for the other shoe to drop. It never did.

"Well, how much should I be spending on shoes and clothes?" Bill's wife, Joan, said. I think she was expecting me to scold her too.

"It's not my budget." I had repeated this phrase multiple times over the last hour. "I just know that, right now, you are spending every dime you make from your paycheck. That's why you're not saving any money." My explanation was simple, but Joan was determined to receive further guidance.

"Well, is there a guideline or something?" she pressed me again.

"Do *you* think you spend too much money on clothes and shoes?" I pressed her back.

"Well, when you lay it out like this and everything we spent money on in a year is shown in one book, everything looks so expensive!" she said, giving me the cue I needed.

"Well, what would be a good amount of money to spend in a month? If we figure that out, then we can figure out how much you can spend on clothes and shoes. How does that sound?"

At that point, the tone of the conversation changed, and we started to get somewhere. We began to work productively on a revised budget that was more in line with what they could afford. It took an hour to get there, but we finally began to make decisions on what could be cut and what couldn't.

Most people are like Bill and Joan. They really don't know how much they spend of their own money. They are mystified by how the money seems to disappear from their account each month. They don't know where it goes. This might be comical, except for the fact that your entire financial life begins with cash flow. If you can get cash flow right, you can achieve your dreams on much less. If you struggle with cash flow, you stay stuck on Step 1 of your financial plan.

While totally foundational, cash flow can be a tricky subject—largely because of what our money represents to us. As with Bill and Joan, money is not just numbers on a sheet. It is mental and emotional. It represents a lifestyle we are accustomed to or purchases that make us feel like we fit into a community. Money represents comfort and safety—the joy of a holiday bonus or the confidence boost of a new outfit.

It is for all these reasons that money is also the source of so much conflict. Cash flow discussions often spark anxiety, fear of not having enough, fear of missing opportunities, or disagreements about how money should be spent. Some clients say they want to talk to me about budgeting, but they are really hoping I'll tell their spouse they're spending too much. If it is a couple like Bill and Joan, one spouse may be upset at the other's spending habits. Now they want me to use my "authority" as a financial advisor to bring down the hammer.

Shaming a client in any way is an unproductive and wrong use of a financial advisor. To many people's shock, a financial advisor cannot tell you how to spend your money. That's not their job. Their job is to help you develop and quantify your goals. If cash flow becomes an issue, their job is to help you make decisions about how much you need to cut and where. However, a financial advisor cannot or should not tell you how much spending in a particular area is too much or not enough.

Why? Because money is fungible—it's mutually interchangeable. Let's say you've budgeted $100 to spend on shoes and $100 to spend on groceries. You only spend $75 on groceries, but you spend $125 on shoes. As a financial advisor, I am still happy with this result. You still only spent $200 overall, and you are still within budget. If you buy $95 in groceries and spend $125 on shoes, then I am not okay with this (and you shouldn't be either). Now you have spent more than your $200 allotment—and you are over budget. You don't get credit for being under budget on groceries if you're spending too much on shoes (or vice versa).

It doesn't matter where you spend it or what budgeting category a purchase belongs in. It's the overall result that matters. If you spend too much overall, then you are sacrificing your long-term financial goals. And the more you do this, the more you sacrifice. At some point, you may have to make some serious trade-offs. For example, you may not be able to retire when you want to or send your children to college. This all comes back to cash flow decisions earlier in life.

Why is cash flow Step 1?

Several years ago, I was asked to appear on a streaming news channel to discuss budgeting. The anchor asked me to describe the best budgeting tip I ever received. I simply said, "Don't spend as much as you take in." The terseness of my answer seemed to take her off guard, but I was being honest. The people who tend to feel like money is always tight are often the same as those who have trouble saving. If you control your spending, money feels less tight. Period. You can absorb unexpected costs (car repairs, sickness, and so on) more easily.[2]

Cash flow and budgeting are the first steps in building a financial plan because they allow you to execute on every other part of the plan. If you manage cash flow well, you are able to build an emergency fund, purchase life insurance, and start funding retirement accounts. If you don't manage cash flow well, you won't be able to afford these things and your financial goals get delayed further and further into the future. It all starts with cash.

I often hear people say they will start saving once they begin to make more money. In my experience, this is typically not the case. If you are not careful with your spending when you are making a modest wage, this behavior generally does not improve as you make more. It is not unusual to see doctors or attorneys, who make plenty of money, struggle with saving and building an emergency fund. Wages are not the problem. It all comes back to spending. If you focus on spending and controlling cash flow, many other problems tend to work themselves out.

How Should You Approach Budgeting?

Controlling cash flow involves discipline—and many people find this a struggle. That's where a budget can help. While the amount spent is more important than what you spent it on, a budget helps us see where our money is going. We have an easier time processing our spending by categories, as opposed to looking at our spending in total. For example, it is easier to see if we spent too much on restaurants by just looking at our credit card bill for the month. It is also easier to see if our electric bill is higher than normal. Our brains simply do better processing smaller categories of expenses rather than just looking at

2 I acknowledge that there are some people who do not make a living wage—even in the richest countries. My statements assume that the person is making a living wage.

the entire budget in total. If we can control our spending in individual categories, we can control our spending overall.

For this reason, you should set up your budget to measure individual line items that tend to occur each month. For example, typical categories include rent, electricity, water, restaurants, cell phone, and gas. For each of these, create three columns: actual amount spent, budgeted amount, and the difference (in other words, the amount over or under budget). Here's an example.

Sample Budget Categories

<Image: Budget Category Example>

You should also have a miscellaneous category for expenses that do not fit well into other categories. It is wise to budget a small amount for unexpected expenses each month. If you do not use this money, it can be added to your savings.

What About Savings?

The most important line item in any budget is savings. You should generally try to save approximately 10 to 15 percent of your income (net pay—that is, after taxes) each month. For example, if your monthly income is $5,000, you should try to save between $500 and $750 each month. Setting this money aside allows you to make progress toward bigger financial goals, like buying a house or saving for retirement.

Why is this the most important line item? It has to do with the time value of money. If you put money into an account that earns interest, you will accumulate additional wealth over time. The key is, however, putting money into the account and *leaving* it there. The more time that money earns interest, the more wealth you will accumulate. Very simply, the sooner you start saving, the more money you will make. The sooner you put money into an interest-bearing account, the longer the timeframe it has to grow.

Let's say I have $1,000 to put into savings. The savings account earns 5 percent per year. If I put the money into savings on January 1, I will have $1,005 at the end of the year on December 31 ($1,000 x 1.05). If I wait and put the money into savings on July 1, then I will only accumulate $1,002.50.[3] This is the difference after six months. What if you wait ten years to begin saving? What about twenty years or more? You miss out on a lot of potential savings and additional interest by waiting to save! The sooner you begin saving, the more money you will accumulate over time. In many ways, it is a race to put money into savings—as much as you can, as soon as you can.

What If I Can't Afford to Save?

I get this question a lot. People don't generally have a problem with the *concept* of saving; they have trouble applying it to their own lives. If this is your situation, put together your budget and look at your actual spending over the last few months. Where is your money going? Review each spending category. Are there surprises? Anything you didn't realize you were spending money on?

As I mentioned earlier, I can't tell you what the appropriate amount is to spend in a particular category. However, I *can* tell you that when I have clients go through this exercise, they are normally surprised to see what they are actually spending money on. They usually don't even realize the cost until they see it added up for each month over a period of time.

Here are some common areas clients tend to feel they are spending too much money on in their own budgets:

---

3 This example ignores compound interest. In real life, savings accounts often do daily or continuous compounding, so the actual amounts would be slightly different. However, the point remains that the sooner you can put money into savings, the more money you will accumulate!

- *Recurring charges & subscriptions*: Recurring charges for streaming services, software subscriptions, and other electronic media are easy to lose track of. We sign up for a service and then forget we have it until we see a charge on our credit card bill. We then say to ourselves, "I should really cancel that," but never get around to it. The cycle then starts over again!

  Make a point of reviewing your automatic subscriptions each month. If you are not using something, cancel it. If you are unsure about one, go ahead and cancel it. See if you miss it. Several years ago, I decided to try not having cable TV. I canceled it and have never renewed. You may be surprised how many subscriptions you really don't need or use!

- *Restaurants & fast food*: We live in a fast-paced, on-the-go society. It's difficult not to spend any money going out to eat. We eat at restaurants and fast food out of convenience. We eat it because we forgot to pack a lunch. We eat it when we are looking to impress someone, or just to spend time with our significant other. Like so many things in budgeting, the key is really moderation and planning.

If you find you are spending too much money at lunch on fast food, try planning out your meals in advance. Spend some time before the work week starts figuring out what you will eat over the next week. If you can, prepare your lunch for each day and label it in the refrigerator. That way, you can just grab the container on your way out the door in the morning (or whenever you are going to work).

Many people go out to eat for lunch during the work week to give themselves a change of scenery. They get tired of seeing their office walls, and they just want a break from their colleagues. Going out serves as an excuse to leave their desk. If this is you, try packing a sandwich from home and going to a nearby park or somewhere away from the office to eat. If this is not a possibility, at the very least, go to a break room and get away from where you normally sit.

Going out to eat every now and again is not a problem for most people. If you plan for it, it becomes much easier to stay within budget.

- *Gas, oil, and car maintenance*: When I was sixteen, my father told me that buying a car was the worst investment I could make. That didn't stop me from saving up from part-time and summer jobs to buy a car as soon as I could. I still love to drive even many years later. The idea of being able to go wherever I want, whenever I want, is still appealing. However, my dad was not wrong. From a financial perspective, cars cost a lot of money. You have routine maintenance costs, state inspection costs, insurance, and personal property taxes. These costs exist, even if you don't have a car loan. They never stop throughout the life of the car.

  One option is to simply give up your car. Before you do this, you should think through other options for transportation. If you live in an area like New York City, it is possible that public transportation may be widely available. You may also be able to take advantage of ride-sharing services (like Uber or Lyft) or taxis. Another option is simply walking (which can help you get a little exercise in the process). However, in addition to thinking through routine situations, you should also consider how you would deal with emergencies that come up. For example, how do you get to the hospital if you don't own a car? If there are enough viable options, you can save a lot of money by simply not owning one.

  In certain situations, this may not be possible. If you live in a more rural area, public transportation may not be as prevalent. In this situation, it may not be possible to completely give up all vehicles—but you may be able to reduce the number you own. For example, you could consolidate to one vehicle. If you live with other people, you could share rides to work, run errands together, or plan to simply use your car less. This will reduce gas, oil, and many routine maintenance costs.[4] If your job allows for it, you may also be able to work remotely. This would cut down on transportation costs to and from work.

It may also be possible to purchase an electric vehicle. Electric vehicles can reduce the amount spent on gasoline. Also, you may be able to take advantage of certain tax incentives. Before buying an electric car, you should explore where charging stations are available. You should also compare the cost of buying an electric vehicle versus buying a gasoline car. Again, the point is that, with a little bit of foresight and planning, there are cost-saving opportunities surrounding transportation.

- *Utilities (including cable, internet, and phone)*: There are often very simple ways to cut down spending on utilities. If you can stand to put on a sweater or sweatshirt in the winter, you can leave the thermostat at a lower temperature. In the summer, you can leave the thermostat a few degrees higher. When you are not at home for extended periods of time or sleeping, it may be ideal to simply turn the thermostat off. While you always want to be mindful of making sure that pipes do not freeze and that there are no issues with heat sickness, controlling the thermostat can be a very easy way to keep utility bills down. Smart thermostats are also controllable through a phone app, which makes them even easier to control regardless of where you are.

  With cable, phone, and internet providers, you may be able to save some money by simply cutting down your services to only what you need. For example, many internet service plans have basic

---

4 It should be noted that long periods where you don't use your vehicle can also be damaging to it. If you are going to own a car, you should continue to maintain it—even if you are using it sparingly!

and advanced plans. If you are not using all services, you may be able to subscribe to a more basic plan. You should also look for deals. Wireless is a highly competitive industry. There may be incentives for periodically shopping services and switching.

If you've exhausted all your options and cannot find another place to cut costs, the only other option is to try to pick up some additional income through a side gig or take on additional work. I always question a client who comes to this conclusion, because it is not often the case that there is truly nothing in the budget that can be trimmed. However, sometimes this is the only conclusion. You free up cash flow by either cutting expenses or creating additional income. If it is not possible to cut expenses, then there is no other choice. You must find ways to save in order to reach financial success.

What If I Am Struggling with Debt?

If you have debt, you want part of your outgoing cash flow to go toward paying it off. In general, you want to pay off higher interest debts first (before lower interest debts). Credit card debts tend to have the highest interest rates, followed by personal loans, car loans, and finally mortgage loans. Paying off credit cards first will allow you to have less interest accumulate each month.

One potential solution to credit card debt is to utilize a balance transfer. This is where you pay a fee to move a balance on one credit card over to another. The idea is that the card you transfer the balance to will have a lower interest rate. Many cards offer promotional balance transfers, such as 0 percent interest on balance transfers for nine months. This can be a way to stop the accumulation of interest for a short period of time. However, most balance transfers have fees—so be careful. Also, be mindful of when the promotional period will end and interest will begin accumulating again.

In some cases, it may be advantageous to pay off credit card debt by taking out a personal loan. Personal loans provide the opportunity to pay a fixed amount each month at a fixed interest rate—which is often lower than the normal credit card interest rate. If you *do* need to take out a loan, look for the lowest rate possible. For example, a car loan may be cheaper through a bank as opposed to buying through the financing arm at the dealer.

Ultimately, the best way to deal with debt is to avoid accumulating it. Avoid making unnecessary big purchases if you don't have the money. As I tell many clients, the best debt is no debt at all—but if you can't have that, be proactive in terms of how you approach paying your debt back.

But I Can't Give That Up!

Perhaps the biggest barrier to proper budgeting is our own mindset. As mentioned, people have emotional connections with money. They associate money with the ability to go to the hair salon every week, take their child out to lunch, and buy name-brand sneakers. We associate money with the ability to do the things we want to do when we want to do them. Money is inherently tied up with comfort and freedom . . . which is why it can be especially difficult to tell ourselves "no."

When I was in Kindergarten, I remember learning about needs and wants. Back then, the examples my teacher gave were black and white. Water and shelter were needs. Nintendo and candy were wants. As you get older, you realize that this line blurs. One's subscription to Netflix doesn't appear to be a need initially. However, I distinctly remember one of my clients who was a single mother saying that her ability to watch old reruns of The Office was one of the few points in her day where she could truly relax. Seeing Dwight K. Schrute talk about his beet farm was more than just comedy, it was a mental break—it helped her get through the week a little easier and gave her a chance to recharge. In this case, it was more accurate to classify Netflix as a need for her mental health.

There is nothing that is inherently wrong to have in a budget. However, not everything you spend money on is equally important. When you look at your budget, you should think about what things are the most important to you and prioritize them. Start with the things you really cannot part with, then rank all the items in your budget. Going through the process of figuring out what is most important to you can help you see where the opportunities are to save money. The items you deem less important are the things you should consider trimming.

Do You Have Any Tips for Making Sure I Don't Go Outside My Budget?

If you are having trouble staying within budget, using more hard cash may help. Set aside in your wallet the specific amount of cash you want to spend—and *only* use that cash. You'll easily see when you are starting to come near your budget limit . . . because you will literally see the cash disappearing from your wallet.

Please note: If you try this method, you should be aware of how much cash you are carrying for security reasons. You don't need to carry your entire budget for the month in your wallet. Only take with you what you need for that particular trip. Leave the rest at home or in a secure spot in your car. You want to stay within budget while not creating a significant security risk.

Where Do I Put My Savings? And What About Retirement?

Once you have successfully freed up cash flow as much as possible, you need to make some choices on where to place your savings.

In general, you want to start by establishing an emergency fund in an account you can pull from if you need it. An emergency fund covers unexpected expenditures, such as car repairs, health care bills, or unplanned travel costs. It also covers living expenses if you lose your job. For this reason, you should keep enough money in your emergency fund to cover how much time it would take you to find a job if you lost your current one. For most people, three months' worth of expenses will be enough. So, if you make $4,000 per month in net pay (after taxes) at your current employer, you should have about $12,000 set aside in an emergency fund.

In certain situations, you may need more emergency fund savings. For example, let's say you work in a highly specialized industry in which jobs are not as plentiful. In this scenario, it may be appropriate to have five or six months of wages set aside. You also need more money in an emergency account if you are an executive. There are very few executive-level jobs available, so it is reasonable to assume that it will take you longer to find one if you are terminated from your current role. Therefore, it is important to give this decision some significant thought. How much time do you think it would take to find a new job? This will dictate how much you should save in an emergency account.

A retirement account is also a highly useful place for long-term savings. Most retirement accounts are 401(k) or 403(b) plans. While 401(k) plans are offered by for-profit employers, you might have a 403(b) plan if you work for a nonprofit, public school, or the government.[5] In both of these plans, though, it is common for the employer contribution to be based on how much you put in. For example, an employer might match dollar-for-dollar on the first 3 percent of employee deferrals. Therefore, if an employee had a paycheck of $2,000 and they

5 There are technical distinctions between 401(k)s and 403(b)s in terms of the types of employers that offer them, what the retirement funds may be invested in, and how much money may be contributed each year to them. However, this is less important for our purposes here. If you need more details here, talk to a CPA or financial advisor.

decided to contribute $60 of this amount (3 percent of $2,000) to the 401(k), the employer would contribute $60 to the employee's account as well. In this scenario, you would not want to contribute anything less than 3 percent of your paycheck—you would want to make sure your employer was contributing as much as possible. Employers can set up retirement plans in various ways with different ways to match contributions, so it's very important to know how your plan works. You should know how much you need to contribute to the 401(k) to get the maximum employer contribution.[6]

It will benefit you to begin saving in both an emergency account and a retirement account as soon as possible. For most people, retirement is the largest expenditure they will ever have. Retirement will cost more than a house or college education, as you're funding several years of your life in advance. With innovations in medical technology, it is not unusual for people to live twenty years or more in retirement.

Retirement savings should begin as soon as possible so you can take advantage of the time value of money. You need as many years as possible to save. You also need to begin saving into an emergency fund right away; you can never be sure when the unexpected might happen. In other words, you need to do both at the same time.

What Is the Right Split Between Emergency Fund Savings and Retirement Savings?

In general, I recommend a 50/50 split between saving for retirement and saving into the emergency fund. That said, if a 50/50 split does not maximize your employer match to retirement, you should adjust this ratio so you are.

---

6 Not every retirement account allows for employee contributions. For example, simplified employee pension (SEP) accounts only allow for employers to make contributions to employee plans. Again, you need to make sure you understand how the retirement plan works at your job, so you can contribute the most possible.

For example, say you can save $200 each month. If you must make a $120 contribution to your retirement account to get the full employer match, you should give $120 to retirement and $80 to the emergency fund. However, if it only takes $100 to get the full employer match, you should put $100 into the 401(k) and $100 into emergency savings. In short, contribute enough to retirement to get the full match, and then save anything left for emergencies. Once you've accumulated enough in emergency savings, you can begin contributing more to retirement funds or begin secondary savings.

What Should I Invest Emergency Savings In?

Emergency savings accounts need to be available when you need them. Therefore, it is often best to utilize online savings, money market, or interest-bearing checking accounts. These accounts are unlikely to lose value and are easily accessible. You can normally withdraw money from them using an ATM card.

Banks may have very different interest rates. It is often best to shop around and look for the one that will give you the highest possible interest rate. You should always pay attention to the bank's fee schedule and any minimum balance requirements. I recommend finding an account without a minimum balance requirement. That way, if you need to drain the account to pay for something big, you will not have to pay a fee.

You should also consider convenience. Online savings accounts may be fine for an emergency bank account—if you can access funds easily. Even a bank that gives you back a higher interest rate may not be helpful if there are no ATMs for you to access the money quickly. Transaction times for emergency accounts should be kept to a minimum in case you run into a situation where you cannot wait three days for a transfer to post to your account. To cut down on transaction times, you can open your main checking account and emergency account at the same bank. If this is the case, transfers between savings and checking accounts are often instantaneous.

Even if you have an emergency savings account, you should also have at least one major credit card available. Credit cards are helpful in rare situations where you need cash for a large expense, like car repairs or unexpected travel costs. You can more easily afford to have a longer transfer time from your emergency account if you have a major credit card. If you need to pay for a large expense, you can use your credit card now and then pay it off in a few days once the transfer from your emergency account posts to your main checking account.

The bottom line: What would you actually need to do logistically if an emergency came up? How would you get the funds you need? How fast would they need to get there? If you think through these questions, you can identify what accounts would be best for emergency savings.

Where Do I Invest My Retirement Funds?

There are several ways to invest for retirement, depending on how much money you want to accumulate in retirement. In general, younger workers should invest more heavily in stocks and other risky investments. Stocks have historically earned a higher rate of return than bonds over a long period of time (thirty years or more). They are also more volatile. This means that prices tend to move up and down more than other types of investments. But when you are younger, you typically have less money to invest anyway. So, a 10 percent drop in the value of your investments may only mean you lose a few dollars. Therefore, it is normally best to invest more heavily in stocks when you are younger.

When you are older and closer to retirement, drops in the market mean more because you have more money saved and invested. A 10 percent drop in the market could mean you lose several thousand dollars or more. For this reason, it is normally best to invest in less volatile investments (like bonds or cash) when you begin nearing retirement age. You want to conserve what you have so you can reach your retirement goals.

Keep in mind: These are only general rules. You should consider your own personal situation and feelings toward the markets and investing before you make any decisions. For example, let's say you receive a large inheritance when you are very young. You may want to invest more conservatively. After all, if you can reach your retirement goals without achieving a high rate of return, why put your money in risky investments? Why take the chance of your investments losing large amounts of value? If you only need to achieve a small rate of return, why not invest in something less volatile and make sure your money is there when you need it?

We will talk more about investing later. For now, remember that there is no one right way to invest for everyone. In general, you should invest in riskier assets when you are younger and the pile of money is lower. But more than anything else, you must be able to sleep at night. As I have told many clients, markets routinely move up and down each day depending on what is going on in our world. We can't stop this from happening. You need to be comfortable with how your money is invested. If it bothers you to see your retirement account decrease in value, you should invest in something more conservative (bonds or other liquid options). You will sleep better and be happier!

What Do the Choices Mean on My Employer Retirement Account?

Most of the time, for an employer retirement account like a 401(k) or 403(b), employees are asked to pick from three investment styles—conservative, moderate, and aggressive. (Some employers may have five or seven options, but the styles are often described in this way.) The aggressive option normally means you are investing more in stocks (80 percent or higher). Conservative investment options typically mean you invest more in bonds and cash. Moderate may be a combination.

Some employers offer retirement options that use target date funds. A target date fund is one that starts off with a heavier allocation of stocks and then gradually adjusts to more bonds over time as the employee gets closer to retirement. The employee will be asked to pick their anticipated retirement year. The more years that they have until retirement, the more stocks will be in the portfolio. In this way, target date funds are fundamentally sound; they take into consideration the general portfolio allocation rules discussed above—moving to more conservative investments later.

The problem with target date funds is that they don't really consider the individual investor. For example, if you are twenty-one years old, just starting to work, and market volatility makes you uncomfortable, a target date fund that is heavily weighted toward stocks may not be appropriate.[7] Therefore, it is best to look at what the actual portfolio will consist of. Companies are required to disclose what makes up each of the portfolio options in their retirement account options. Given the issues discussed above, you should pick the one that works best for you.

Back to Budgeting . . . How Do I Know If I Have It Right?

In most cases, I tell clients to review their budgets every six months unless they have a major life change (in which case they may have to review sooner). Major life changes are anything that dramatically changes someone's financial life. Having a new child, moving into a new home, or taking a new job are a few examples of common events

---

7 Incidentally, this can also be a problem with the investment style options as well. For example, the aggressive portfolio may have too much volatility for the employee, but the moderate portfolio is too conservative. In this way, neither may be an ideal fit.

that can significantly change how one budgets due to having more expenses, more money, or some combination of both.

Except in these scenarios, you want to check your budget every six months to make sure it still makes sense and you are not missing significant expenses. Budgets should be tight, but also realistic. Yours should generally incorporate all your recurring expenses for a particular period. If it does not, the budget should be revised.

As I have told many clients, budgets create spending awareness. Like my clients Bill and Joan learned that day in my office, there is not necessarily an objectively right or wrong way to spend your money. The key is to be aware of where your money is going, so you can analyze and take control of it. You can ensure that you are not spending too much in areas you don't intend. You can also make sure you are saving enough. If you are staying within budget and saving consistently, you can begin to accumulate wealth. However, this all begins with mastering your day-to-day cash flow. You can't invest toward your future unless you get control over today.

Key Takeaways

1. If you want to build your financial future, you must begin with your day-to-day cash flow. Once you master that, you can start building your emergency savings and retirement accounts.
2. A good budget needs to fit you and what you spend your money on. It should be tight but realistic. Review your budget every six months and compare it to actual spending. Adjust as needed.
3. Savings is the most important item in any budget. If you need additional funds in both retirement and your emergency fund, you should split this budgeted savings roughly 50/50 between the two.

4. Emergency funds should be accessible to you if something happens. Keeping an emergency credit card available can be a safeguard so you don't need to have cash immediately available.
5. While there are many retirement account options available, make sure you're meeting any requirements to get the full employer match and that the investments you choose are consistent with your own risk tolerance.

STEP 2

Once You Have Something, Protect It

"I don't know how we are going to get out of this."

I was staring at an imperfection in the wood floor near my feet when she said this. I didn't need to look at her face to know what she was feeling. I could hear it in her voice.

"We worked hard and saved. Now one bad day. And now I am trying to figure out how many more days he can stay."

The toughest job I ever had was being a hospital chaplain. I went from one hard conversation to another. Before I started, I always assumed that chaplains basically spent all day talking about God, theology, and the meaning of life. Nothing was further from the truth. I spent more time just listening to people's pain—trying to help them understand why they had to keep going. This type of situation was always the toughest. The United States has some of the best hospitals in the world, but they are also tremendously expensive and insurance eventually runs out. The woman I was talking to that day was tired of fighting.

Her husband had been a contractor for several years. He had always had minor scrapes, aches, and pains, but never anything major. He didn't want to pay for insurance, and he always took notice of his surroundings on the job site. One day, he just had one misstep while on a ladder. Now here we were—me staring a hole into the floor and his wife feeling hopeless. I offered to stay there until the doctor came back. That was really all we could do. We made small talk about the weather, the Pittsburgh Steelers, and even why early Rolling Stones albums were better than the new stuff. However, it was distracted conversation. After an hour or so, I left her wondering if I had done any good or not.

There are many insurance commercials out there with goofy mascots, catchphrases, and gimmicks. They always say something about peace of mind and losing what you have. However, my conversation with a woman in a hospital waiting room that day was no commercial. It was real life. The problem is that not protecting what you have is never a problem—until it is. It is never something that keeps us up at night—until it is. It is never too late to plan for the future—until it is. That's why Step 2, on asset protection, should quickly follow Step 1. Once you have a handle on cash flow, you must begin thinking about insurance and wills.

Don't I Already Have Insurance?

Certain types of insurance are required. For example, most state laws mandate that you have auto insurance to drive a car.[8] Also, many apartment complexes require you to have renters' insurance to protect your belongings. The problem is that checking the box and meeting the requirement may be considerably different from what you need. Many people are surprised to discover the things that are *not* covered under their policies. For example, liability-only auto insurance often has very cheap rates because it provides the least amount of coverage. It might meet the state minimum requirements, but it only covers bodily

8 There is one state that does not technically require auto insurance, but most states require it. And even if it is not required, it is not smart to be driving around without insurance!

injury to others and the property damage that results when you cause an accident. If a tree were to fall on your car, it would not be covered. You would need to pay for the damage the tree caused out of your own pocket.

Am I saying that you need the highest level of coverage? Absolutely not. However, we are all wired differently. Some of us want to make sure we are as covered as much as we can possibly be when an accident happens. Others of us are okay with taking a risk or two if we can save a few bucks now. The key is knowing what you have and what you don't have. Once you have cash flow figured out, you should take a harder look at your insurance policies. Make sure you are aware of and okay with the risks you are taking on. If you have taken care of cash flow and you need more coverage, you now have the money to get it.

Which Types of Insurance Do I Need to Prioritize First?

Just like anything else in your financial life, you often don't have the cash flow to afford everything you need to protect your assets all at once. Therefore, if you are like most people, you will need to prioritize which financial products you buy first—and which ones to buy later. If you can't afford everything, here is the recommended order for buying the products we will discuss in this chapter:

1. *Health Insurance*: You need to take care of your body and mind and make sure you're able to pay for the care your body needs. Your health is an important asset!
2. *Auto Insurance*: Besides the high frequency of car accidents, it is against the law in nearly every state to drive without any form of auto insurance.
3. *Homeowners/Renters' insurance*: In most cases, landlords require tenants to have renters' insurance. While going without

homeowners insurance may be possible in rare instances, most mortgage companies will require a homeowner to have it as well.

4. *Disability Insurance*: While people tend to ignore the possibility of becoming disabled, a twenty-year-old has a one in four chance of becoming disabled before retirement.[9]
5. *Life Insurance*: Just because life insurance is at the bottom of the list does not mean it isn't important. As we will discuss, it's something most people want for the sake of their loved ones or legacy. Plus, it's generally less expensive if you buy it when you're younger. However, your chances of dying in a given year are much less than the chances of you getting sick (health insurance) or becoming disabled (disability insurance). Therefore, if one of these items must be put off, it should probably be the purchase of life insurance.

Now that we have a roadmap for protecting your assets, we need to talk about two important concepts that will come into play in nearly every insurance policy you buy—deductibles and coverage limits.

Why Are Deductibles Important?

If something is covered, it is covered. Right?

Not exactly. An insurance deductible is the amount you pay out of your own pocket before the insurance company starts paying. For example, let's say your policy has a $500 deductible. Your car has $1,500 in damages. You would pay the first $500 out of your own pocket to get the car repaired. The additional $1,000 would be paid by insurance.

If you have a higher deductible, you will pay less for your insurance. However, that also means you will owe more money if a claim

9 Tiffany Bosley and Johanna Maleh, "*Disability and Death Probability Tables for Insured Workers Who Attain Age 20 in 2022*" (Social Security Administration, December 2022), https://www.ssa.gov/oact/NOTES/ran6/an2022-6.pdf.

happens. If you have an ample emergency fund, you may be able to get by with a higher deductible on your insurance policy. If you do get into an accident, you can simply use those savings (and then replenish the emergency fund as soon as possible). If you have trouble saving money, though, it is important to keep lower deductibles so you don't empty your entire account in the case of an accident.

Not every insurance policy has a deductible. For example, a life insurance policy does not. However, property and casualty insurance policies, like renters, homeowners, and auto insurance, nearly always do. Also, health insurance policies often have an amount that you must pay on prescriptions, doctor visits, and hospitalizations before your insurance will pick up the tab (called a co-pay). Therefore, it is important to know what a deductible is when you see it on your policy!

How Much Coverage Is Enough?

So after my deductible, insurance will pay for everything else?

Again, not quite. There is another important piece of an insurance policy: a coverage limit. The coverage limit is the highest amount the insurance company will pay in case of an accident. When selecting this number, you want to secure enough coverage so that even in the case of an accident, you will not reach that ceiling.

How do you know if your coverage limit is high enough? This is the magic question. The technical answer: You should get enough insurance to cover your needs. For example, in the case of auto insurance, you should buy enough to cover the worst accident you can envision. If the most damage you could ever cause in an accident is $100,000, you should get $100,000 worth of coverage. In the case of life insurance, how much money would your family and loved ones need if you passed away?

While this formula is simple in theory, this number is actually quite difficult to figure out. How do you know what your needs really are?

For property and casualty insurance policies, like auto, homeowners, and renters' insurance, it may be helpful to simplify the problem. You should always get coverage for property equal to the value of that property. In other words, get enough coverage to cover the replacement value of the car, house, boat, or any other property you might own.

Liability coverage is trickier. It is often best to think about how much you would be willing to pay out of pocket for an accident that was your fault. If you never want to pay anything out of pocket, it is best to get the greatest amount of coverage possible. If you are okay with the thought of paying something out of pocket for a large enough claim, then a lower package might be okay. As a financial advisor, I always tell clients to guess high. You might be surprised at how much a claim truly costs!

For health and disability insurance, evaluating your own needs is more complex. But before we try to answer that question, we need to gain an understanding of the difference between the two policies.

What's the Difference Between Health Insurance and Disability Insurance?

While health insurance and disability insurance may appear similar on the surface, they cover very different things. Health insurance is meant to cover treatment costs for physical issues, along with some mental health issues as well. Health insurance generally reimburses or covers the actual cost of treatment. If the bill for your treatment is $100, insurance might cover $65 of it. Many routine or annual treatments are covered through health insurance, like annual physicals.[10]

Disability insurance, on the other hand, is meant to cover the

10 We don't say too much here about dental and vision coverage, but they often act similarly to health insurance. Routine exams (like semi-annual teeth cleanings or annual eye exams) are often covered. Specialized care may be covered, but only up to a certain point.

income lost when a person becomes disabled and is unable to work. It does *not* cover any specific treatment, medical bills, or additional expenses a person may have due to disability. (Beyond these basic differences, we'll discuss disability insurance more later.)

I Never Know Which Health Insurance To Pick During Open Enrollment.

The number of options and features when it comes to health insurance can be overwhelming. In many cases, people get health insurance through their employer. Thus, they're prompted each year to renew their health coverage decision at open enrollment. Employers may offer one health plan or many, but your decision should ultimately come down to finding the plan that covers what you need.

1. To start, you should check whether trips to your main doctor (primary care physician) will be covered under the plan. If you get your annual physical at their office, would this be a covered expense?
2. Second, does the plan cover any regular prescriptions you use?
3. Third, consider the mental health professionals, chiropractors, and others who help maintain your well-being. Think about all the professionals you see on a regular basis. Are visits to them covered under the plan? If they are not covered, then how will you get this care? Would you be willing to pay out of pocket? If so, you need to incorporate this into your budget (see Step 1).

Aside from seeing if these core items are covered, you should also pay attention to deductibles and how much of the premium is covered by your employer. Deductibles can add up quickly if you have regular expenses like medications. Also, if your employer only covers a minimal percentage of the cost, insurance premiums can take a large chunk out of your paycheck. The key is to review these things *before* you receive your first paycheck, so it's not a surprise.

If you want to save a few dollars and do not go to the doctor that often, a health savings account (HSA) may work well for you. An HSA is a tax-deferred savings account for medical expenses. You (or your employer or both) put money into the HSA. The money grows tax-free over time. You can then pull from the account to cover your medical costs.[11]

With an HSA, you must have a high-deductible health plan.[12] While you can use funds from your health savings account to cover this deductible, funds must have had a chance to accumulate in the account first. For example, let's say you have just started contributing to your HSA. The balance in the account will be zero (or very close to it). If you were to get sick right away, you would need to pay for treatment from your own pocket (since no HSA funds would be available). Therefore, it is best to open an HSA when you already have some savings in an emergency account or another source. It is also best if you are someone who resists going to the doctor a bit. As my mother would say, if you cough twice and need to go to the doctor, then an HSA is probably not right for you!

In all seriousness, a health savings account is not for everyone, but it can work well for certain people. Many employers offer an HSA (though not all). If you are self-employed, you also may be able to take advantage of an HSA in the marketplace when you buy your health insurance.

Remember—even if you don't choose an HSA, you just need to know if your health insurance will cover your needs and how much it will cost, so you can budget accordingly. One way to do this is to figure

---

11 If you use money out of an HSA to cover a cost that is not medical-related, you normally will need to pay a tax penalty.

12 What constitutes a high-deductible health plan is defined by the IRS each year. The IRS will say what the maximum out-of-pocket and minimum deductible must be for a plan to be considered a "high-deductible health plan."

out how much it would cost you each year for each plan for routine medical expenses that you know you would have. For example, how much would an annual physical cost? What about a trip to the dentist for your semi-annual teeth cleaning? Then think through what happens if you are hospitalized. Would that be covered? How much would that cost you out of pocket under each plan? While this is not a single amount of coverage that is right for everyone, you can think through some scenarios to help you get a handle on which plan is best. If you are not sure how to actually compute the cost, a benefits specialist, HR professional, or financial advisor can help.

The real secret to making the best choices for your health insurance is this: *Don't just pick something.* When I first started working, I had a friend who always picked the same health insurance option each year at open enrollment. She never looked at what the plan covered or whether or not her doctor was in the provider network. She hated the open enrollment meeting and often complained about it being boring and a waste of time. In an effort to get away from this verbal torture, she would simply mark the box that said "no changes." This worked well for years until she ended up in the hospital. Some of the tests ran by the doctors were not covered, and she ended up shocked with a pile of medical bills. The point here: Take a few minutes to understand your policy. If you are not sure if something is covered, ask your HR administrator or call the insurance company. A few minutes can save you a lot of headaches!

Auto Insurance and the Maze of Mascots

"What does an emu or a gecko have to do with insurance?" my friend exclaimed as he shook his head at the TV.

"Well, I mean, it's entertaining," I said meekly with a shrug. Clearly, I was not sharing the utter disdain for commercials pedaling auto insurance that my friend was.

"No, I am being serious. Is this supposed to make me buy insurance? How do I navigate the maze of mascots to figure out what policy is best?"

No other industry seems to use comedy so effectively to market something ordinary as the auto insurance industry. If you are like most people, you laugh at the commercials—but like my friend, you wonder if you are really getting the best deal for your auto insurance. After all, the commercial that makes you laugh the hardest probably isn't the best way to pick your policy. So how should you choose?

My biggest tip for anyone looking for auto insurance is don't be afraid to shop around—and don't ever think rates are approximately the same. Auto insurance is a state-mandated product, which means insurance companies must structure their policies in accordance with certain requirements. One may handle claims better than another or have better customer service, but there is no difference in the actual *quality* of a policy from a name-brand insurance company and a lesser-known one. Also, some insurance companies have better rates in particular regions of the country. Don't automatically assume you're getting the best deal.

Brand loyalty isn't necessarily rewarded in the auto insurance industry either. Just because you have been a customer for a long time, it doesn't mean you are getting the best deal. In fact, as long as an insurance company is meeting the laws of your state, they can price their policies more cheaply for new customers—and higher for those that are renewing. Ever notice how your insurance company is typically hounding you well in advance of your policy renewing? That may be because they want you to renew—and not look around for a cheaper rate.

The only way to ensure you have the best deal is to shop around. You may be missing out! I typically recommend shopping for your auto insurance policy once every two or three years. However, when you are looking around, you need to make sure that you are still getting the right amount of coverage. If you take on less coverage, you will normally get a cheaper rate—but it may not cover you if you are in an accident.

What Are the Three Numbers on an Insurance Policy?

Like many other financial products, auto insurance has its own language. Insurance companies will often use shorthand to say how much coverage a person has. Common coverage amounts include the following:

- 25/50/25
- 50/100/25
- 100/300/50
- 250/500/100

The first two numbers represent the liability coverage for bodily injury that you cause to another person. The last number is the amount of liability coverage you have for damage to others' property. For example, if you have 100/300/50 coverage, it means your coverage for bodily injury you cause is $100,000 per person up to $300,000 per accident. In this example, you have $50,000 of coverage for any property damage you cause.

Therefore, let's say you hit another car with four people in it, and you were responsible for $100,000 in injuries for each person in the other car (so $400,000 in total).[13] Your insurance company would only cover $300,000 of the injuries—not the full $400,000 you owe. This is because while the policy has a per-person liability limit of $100,000, it also has a per-accident limit of $300,000. If the damage were below these limits, you would have to pay your deductible, but insurance would pick up the rest.

---

13 Injuries covered by auto liability insurance may include legal fees, funeral costs, and pain and suffering, in addition to the medical expenses of another person.

What Other Types of Auto Insurance Can Protect Me in an Accident?

While you can buy liability-only insurance, that type of insurance only covers the other person's expenses in an accident where you are at fault. But what about your expenses? Or what if you are not at fault, and the other person does not have enough insurance to cover your costs? What if no one is at fault? Additional coverage can address each of these scenarios.

- *Uninsured motorist coverage*: This covers damage to you and your car if you are hit by another motorist who does not have insurance (or whose insurance company is insolvent). It also covers a hit-and-run accident (in which the person who hit you flees the scene).
- *Underinsured motorist coverage:* While the names sound similar, *un*insured and *under*insured coverages are quite different. Underinsured coverage applies to a situation in which the other person who hit you *has* coverage, but it is not enough to cover the accident.
- *Damage to your auto (collision coverage)*: This covers damage to your automobile regardless of whether you are at fault for the accident.
- *Damage to your auto (other than collision):* This coverage reimburses you for damage to your vehicle caused by something other than a collision—like a tree limb falling on your car. It is not caused by a crash, but it certainly causes damage!

Forgoing some coverage can save you a few dollars. But be aware that you need to pay for any damage that is not covered under your policy. This may mean you need to pull from your emergency fund. If you don't have an emergency fund, you may need to take out a loan. Again, the point is to be aware of what you have and what you don't, so you can decide what level of risk is best for you.

Isn't Homeowners Included with My Auto Insurance?

In the myriad of television commercials for insurance that you see, you often hear about bundling. Most often, insurance companies are touting the virtues of bundling your home (or renters) insurance with your auto insurance policy. They point to the money that you will save and the ease of having all of your policies with them. The premise of bundling is so prevalent that I have even had a client or two convinced that their auto and homeowners policies were actually just one policy!

I distinctly remember a friend of mine being so convinced of this that she bet me lunch that she was right. She brought her policy with her and walked into my office confidently the next day. She began to rifle through the stack of papers, pointing to how the insurance company name was the same on all the pages. Once she was done, I simply showed her the two declaration pages in her stack of papers—one for auto and one for homeowners. She sheepishly looked up from the mountain of papers now in disarray that she had placed on my desk. Without another word, she simply said, "So where am I taking you for lunch?" I simply smiled and told her that fast food was fine.

It is important to recognize that your auto and home policies are indeed two different policies. While it can be easier to have everything with one company, it is much harder to leave a company if you have to cancel two policies, rather than just one—and the insurance companies know that. This means that customers who have two policies generally stay longer—and the companies collect more premiums, even if they don't have the best rates.

Don't always assume the bundle is better. Check rates and shop your policies every so often. You might be surprised that you are actually paying a higher rate than if you just bought each one separately!

What Does Homeowners Insurance Cover?

It is very difficult (if not impossible) not to have some type of insurance policy on your home. Homeowners coverage is multifaceted because you are covering the cost of damage to your home in addition to covering the contents in it. In general, you want to have coverage that is equal to the value of your home. Contents coverage is typically included as a part of the standard policy.

Many people are surprised to learn that homeowners coverage may not cover high-value items inside your home. For example, let's say you own expensive jewelry, one-of-a-kind artwork, or even a priceless collection of baseball cards. While the standard homeowners policy will provide *some* coverage, it will not cover the full value. A separate policy may be needed to cover the value of items like these.[14] You may also need a separate policy to cover motorcycles, boats, or other types of unique equipment.

Today, it is also not unusual for people to work from home. You may need a separate business policy to cover your home-based business. This is especially true if you see clients in your home or you have special business equipment. Most homeowners policies have little (if any) coverage for business activities. They are made for the personal use of your residence only.

What About Renters' Insurance?

If you rent, you typically want to have a renters policy, which covers the personal belongings inside your home—furniture, electronics, household items, and so on. You don't need to worry about covering the apartment, condo, or house itself, as this is covered under the owner's insurance policy. Rather, the renters' insurance would cover the value

---

14 This separate policy is often an inland marine insurance policy. The insurance company will actually create a schedule of your valuable items and have you agree to a value for these items should they need to be replaced.

of the items you own in the case of something like fire, theft, or water damage. It may also help cover your lodging and meal expenses if your home becomes uninhabitable for whatever reason.

A renter's policy should have coverage equal to the value of the items you own. Estimates are okay, but as I have told clients, you should generally estimate high. It's always better to have a little too much coverage than not enough. The price difference is normally not much for a few thousand dollars more coverage.

While renters' insurance is good for protecting your assets, it may also be required under your lease agreement. This reduces your landlord's own liability. In many cases, landlords insist on a certain amount of coverage—like $50,000 or $100,000. While these limits may seem high, they normally are not. Wedding rings, electronics, and artwork tend to have a high value that can easily exceed lower coverage levels.

The biggest thing to remember for both homeowners and renters' insurance is to review your coverage each year before you renew. Most people accumulate more belongings every year. Values of homes may go up substantially from one year to the next. It's important to adjust your coverage each year to make sure your insurance is still at an adequate level to cover the value of your property.

Do I Really Need Disability Insurance?

Early on in my teaching career, I remember asking this question to a room full of students: "Which is more likely—becoming disabled or dying?"

Very quickly, one of them corrected me. "You didn't mean to ask it that way. Everyone dies. They don't all become disabled."

I realized what I had done. Of course, there is a 100 percent chance that each of us will one day die. I said the only thing I could: "Nothing like embarrassing yourself in front of lots of people."

I rephrased my question the way I meant to ask it: "Which is more likely—becoming disabled or dying—*in any given year up until one retires*?"

The response to this question was much less certain.

"Becoming disabled, I guess," another student offered, which was correct. Yet many people don't understand how common disability is. While everyone is certain about death, they are much less aware of how often disability can change our lives and our families' lives.

Remember what we said earlier: Health insurance reimburses and covers the cost for specific medical expenses; disability insurance covers the loss of income you experience when you become disabled. The disability insurance coverage is based solely on a person's earnings prior to the disability. The more a person earns, the bigger the disability insurance payout will be if a claim happens.

Disability Insurance Myths

Over the years, I have heard many common client myths about disability insurance. Before we discuss why you need disability insurance and how much you need, let's discuss a few of these:

Myth 1: I have disability insurance through my employer, so I don't need to buy any.

It is true that many people have some form of disability insurance through their employer. However, just having disability insurance doesn't mean it is enough. Many employer disability insurance policies will cover about 50 percent of your paycheck if you become disabled.[15] Therefore, the question is not *if* you have disability insurance. The question is: Could you really live on approximately half of your

15 Obviously, some employer policies will offer a higher percentage of wages to be covered than others. The important point here again is to be aware of how much coverage you would really have if you were to become disabled!

paycheck if you were to become disabled? If you can, then the coverage provided through your employer may be fine. If you can't, you may need to buy some additional insurance.

Myth 2: I can get disability insurance coverage through Social Security.

The Social Security system in the United States does offer disability insurance. However, to reap the benefits, you must meet several requirements. According to the Social Security Administration (2024) website: "We consider you disabled under Social Security rules if all of the following are true:

- You cannot do the work that you did before because of your medical condition.
- You cannot adjust to other work because of your medical condition.
- Your disability has lasted or is expected to last for at least one year or to result in death."

In addition, you must have enough quarters of coverage (QCs) through the Social Security system to qualify as disability insured. In general, this means you must have earned a minimum amount of wages (or self-employment income) in the prior ten years to gain access to benefits.[16]

The bottom line is that it is very difficult to qualify for Social Security disability benefits. You can't engage in any gainful employment. In fact, many Social Security disability benefits get denied on the first try. When this happens, there is an appeals process—but it can

16 Technically, the requirement is that you need to have at least twenty QCs in the last ten years. A QC is a minimum amount of wages or self-employment income necessary to get "credit" for Social Security purposes. The amount necessary to obtain a QC is adjusted for inflation each year, so it is not a standard amount. However, in 2024, you would have needed to have at least $1,730 in wages or self-employment income to get one QC.

take some time to work through. Finally, even if the claim is accepted, you generally must wait five months before you begin receiving benefits. Even in the best scenario (the claim is accepted), you will still need to cover your living expenses for five months using savings or other funds available to you. That's a long time! It is often unwise to count on Social Security to provide benefits if you need them.

Myth 3: I won't ever become disabled (or the chances are so small that coverage is not worth it).

Let's hope this one is true. But the problem is that if you *do* happen to become disabled and you are not prepared, it can be an enormous drain on your financial resources. The fact is that becoming disabled is more common than you might think. No one is bullet-proof or accident-proof; to pretend otherwise is simply unrealistic.

How much you need is often a matter of figuring out how much is necessary to live comfortably if you become disabled. You need to look at how much your employer would cover. If that is less than what you can live off, you can either make up the difference by utilizing savings or buying a supplemental disability policy.

Can I Just Get a Policy That Covers 100 Percent of My Paycheck?

Most likely, no. It is unlikely that an insurance company (even one offering supplemental disability insurance benefits) will be willing to write a policy that covers 100 percent of your paycheck. The reason for this is simple. If disability will allow you to receive the same amount of benefits as you would receive if you were working, why go back to work? They want to incentivize you to go back to work if possible.

Another reason is that no one actually receives 100 percent of their paycheck anyway. Think about it. You have taxes taken out of your paycheck, and part of it goes to the government. Insurance companies know this as well, so they certainly don't want you taking home *more* money on disability than you typically would.

Supplemental disability insurance policies are available on the open market from insurance companies. In general, with the addition of a supplemental policy, you might be able to cover 70 to 80 percent of your wages. This depends on finding an insurance company willing to write this policy and your willingness to pay for as much coverage as possible. Obviously, the more coverage you want, the higher the premium you need to pay.

Why Is Disability Insurance so Expensive?

This is a common question I hear because, for some reason, people often expect disability insurance to cost about the same as life insurance. Again, these are two different insurance products, so the insurance company prices them differently. When figuring out the price of any insurance product, insurance companies generally consider three things: average claims cost, their administrative and servicing costs for that policy, and their profit margin. These three components combined determine the premium the customer pays.[17] If any of these components increase, the cost of the policy goes up as well.

In the vocabulary of the insurance industry, a disability insurance claim is often a "long-tail" claim. This means there can be a series of payments made by the insurance company to the insured over a time period. In contrast, life insurance claims are only paid out when a person passes away. While I have never experienced it myself, I believe you can only die once! So, with more payouts and higher claims costs, disability claims end up being more expensive for the insurance companies. It makes sense then that disability insurance is normally more expensive than life insurance.

---

17 In real life, it isn't quite this easy. Insurance companies need to figure out what people are willing to pay, how much investment returns will be, and several other factors. However, in broad strokes, this is roughly correct.

What Should I Keep in Mind When Reviewing My Disability Insurance?

Aside from looking at the amount that would be paid out in the event of a claim, you should review *when* benefits are paid. In general, there are two different types of disability policies—"own occupation" policies and "any occupation" policies. As the names imply, own occupation policies will pay benefits when one is unable to work in their chosen field or profession. An any occupation policy means someone is unable to work in "any occupation." For example, let's say you are a construction worker who becomes injured. The doctor tells you that you are no longer able to do construction, but you can find a job answering phones and doing paperwork for a housing contractor. If you had an own occupation policy, the policy would pay you disability benefits because you are unable to work in your own construction occupation. In contrast, an any occupation policy would not pay benefits because you are still able to perform tasks in a different line of work.

Additionally, many supplemental disability insurance policies require you to maintain your underlying coverage. For example, let's say you work for an employer whose group disability insurance policy (your primary insurance policy) covers 50 percent of your wages, but you want more coverage. Your supplemental insurance policy covers an additional 20 percent of your wages, but it has a clause that requires you to maintain that underlying coverage. You leave your employer to start your own company and no longer maintain a primary disability insurance policy. Then, you get injured. Your supplemental disability insurance will only cover the lost income that it was underwritten for—the 20 percent of wages. But since the initial 50 percent of wages is no longer being covered by your company's policy, you now need to cover it out of pocket. For this reason, if you do purchase disability insurance, you should pay attention to any underlying policies you are required to maintain. The difference in how much you are on the hook for could be substantial!

It should be noted that even if you don't do physical work, you can still become disabled. For example, let's say you work at home on a computer each day. You could still lose your eyesight or have issues with tendons in your hands. While the sources of your injuries may not be the same as a construction worker's, it is still possible for you to have a disability insurance claim.

Finally, we should mention that a common reason for a disability insurance claim is maternity leave. You may be able to receive part of your paycheck while you are recovering from childbirth. However, it is always a wise idea to talk to your employer or a disability insurance specialist so you know what is covered and what is not, as well as when coverage starts (in the weeks leading up to childbirth or after childbirth). Some costs may be covered under health insurance, while your lost wages may be covered under your disability insurance. Also, certain states have laws that mandate parental leave.

That said, navigating this area can be difficult, and the topic is much more complex than this book can satisfy. So, it is important to ask your employer about what benefits you are entitled to before you are out on leave. If you need more information on state-mandated leave programs or supplemental policies you bought on the open market, you should talk to your financial advisor or a specialist in the area.

Do I Need Life Insurance Too?

Now that we have covered health, auto, homeowners, renters, and disability insurance, let's discuss the final stop on our protection roadmap: life insurance. The very fact of life insurance speaks to the truth that we do not know what our future will hold—or how long that future will be. But in the meantime, many of us have loved ones to support or a legacy we'd like to leave behind. Life insurance is a way of making sure each of those wishes becomes a reality when we are no longer around to make them so.

While there are several potential uses for life insurance, in many cases, life insurance is meant to make up for the income your beneficiaries miss out on because of your death. If you have children, your children depend on your income. If you are married, your spouse might depend on your paycheck for the same reason. Without it, they may not be able to pay the mortgage, maintain the household, or pay for childcare. Life insurance would continue providing them the income you could no longer earn for them.

If you are unmarried and have no one who depends on your income, a case can be made that you don't need life insurance. However, that may not be true for you. Life insurance is a very versatile product. It can be used to transfer business interests, even out inheritances, pay off debts, and even leave legacy gifts. Let's say you want to leave one big gift to your favorite charity or school when you pass away. You may be able to leave hundreds of thousands of dollars to a charity or person while only paying a few hundred or a few thousand dollars in premiums. What if you want to leave your house to a friend or family member, but the house is tied up by a mortgage? You could purchase a life insurance policy large enough to allow the person who inherits the house to pay it off.

Life insurance can be very tax-efficient as well. In many situations, the recipient of life insurance proceeds does not need to pay taxes on the amount they receive.[18] So while it is possible that a person may not *need* life insurance, people often use it to accomplish their financial goals.

How Much Life Insurance Do I Need?

This is a tricky question because the amount you need depends on what you are planning to use it for. If you want to give a big, charitable

18 This is not always the case. There are certain situations where life insurance proceeds are taxable. For example, if an employer pays for life insurance premiums and you are the beneficiary on the policy. This may actually result in taxable proceeds to you.

gift to someone at the end of your life, the amount you need is simply the amount you want to give. If you want to give $500,000 at the end of your life to your church or synagogue, you will need a $500,000 policy. If you are trying to leave enough to cover a debt (like a mortgage), you will need life insurance in an amount equal to the debt you are trying to cover. If the mortgage has a balance of $200,000, you will need life insurance of $200,000. These situations are pretty straightforward.

It may be more difficult to figure out how much insurance will cover the needs of a loved one, like a child or spouse, if you pass away. In this instance, you need to think about what expenses they'd still need to cover. And when a person dies, those household expenses do not get cut in half. Family members still need to pay 100 percent of the mortgage, 100 percent of the electric bill, 100 percent of the cable bill, and 100 percent of property insurance—just to name a few. Life insurance is meant to cover the years you would have continued to work if you were still living. So, if you plan to retire in twenty years, you should ideally purchase insurance to cover these expenses for your family or beneficiaries for the next twenty years.

Obviously, this is still a complex calculation. For this reason, many financial advisors have rules of thumb. I often tell clients who do not want to formally calculate how much they need to take their yearly salary and multiply it by ten (essentially assuming that after ten years, your beneficiaries will have adjusted financially to you no longer being there). In general, though, it is always best to have more insurance rather than less.

This Sounds Expensive. What If I Can't Afford It?

In general, if you want more money to be left to your beneficiaries, you need to pay a higher premium. However, if you can't afford the insurance amount you need, the best thing to do is simply pay for what you can and get as close to the amount of coverage you need as possible. Then purchase more coverage in the future.

That said, there are a few other variables that may be able to make your plan cheaper:

- *Term policies are generally cheaper when you are younger.* The chance of you passing away is statistically smaller, so there is a lower chance that the insurance company will have to pay a claim. Starting now with a term plan may actually be a way to save money now and in the long run.
- *A policy for someone who does not smoke usually costs less than a policy for someone who does.* Insurance companies know smoking greatly reduces one's life expectancy, meaning the company will likely need to pay a claim sooner. Knocking this habit is another way to save.
- *Paying each year is generally cheaper than paying by the month (or another shorter interval).* Insurance companies normally charge an installment fee for processing your payment each month. If you pay your premiums annually, you normally do not need to pay this installment fee.

What Is the Difference Between Term and Permanent Insurance Policies?

There are two main categories of life insurance—term and permanent policies. Term policies are exactly what they sound like. They provide coverage for a certain amount of time (a "term") such as one year, five years, ten years, or longer. After the term is over, the policy will need to be renewed for another term for coverage to stay in force.

Let's say you have a five-year, $100,000 term insurance policy. If you pass away during those five years, the policy will pay your beneficiaries $100,000. If you do not renew the policy and you die after six years, your beneficiaries receive nothing. The policy will only pay out a benefit if coverage is in force during the policy term.

Something to keep in mind about term policies is that the premium amount increases each time you renew your policy. Why? As morbid as it is to say, with each renewal, you are closer to death—and the insurance company is closer to paying a claim. Keeping with the example above, your premium would stay the same throughout your five-year term policy. But if you were to renew for another five years, your premium would be higher for the next five years. Some insurance companies will write a term policy that is twenty, twenty-five, or thirty years—leaving your premium steady for quite a long time. But when the time comes that you do need to renew, the premium goes up—sometimes drastically.

In contrast to a term policy, a permanent policy covers one's entire life. There are several types of permanent policies available, but the most popular one is a whole life policy. With whole policy, the premium amount never changes. There is also no need to for the rest of one's life.[19]

Two other noteworthy permanent policies are universal life and variable policies. A universal life policy generally allows for flexible premium payments within certain parameters. As long as the owner of the policy pays the minimum amount, the policy will stay in force. The owner has the option of paying more into the policy to increase its cash value (more on this in a second). Variable life insurance policies have an investment component to them. In general, the death benefit may increase or decrease depending on how the markets perform during the period the policy is in force. A variable universal life policy combines the flexible premiums of a universal life policy with the investment component of a variable life policy.

19 Technically, many whole life policies only cover one up until a particular age, like 110 or 120. Most people don't live that long, though, so we simply say that coverage is good for one's entire life.

Also, in contrast to term, permanent policies generally have a cash value. The owner of the policy can borrow against the cash value of the policy. For example, let's say you own a whole life policy with a $100,000 cash value. You take a loan of $20,000 against this policy, because you need money to pay off a credit card debt or a personal loan. If you die, your beneficiaries would receive $20,000 less (plus any interest that may have accumulated on the loan). The insurance company pays itself back before it pays your beneficiaries.

This is not to say that one should never take out a loan on a life insurance policy. The cash value of a whole life policy might be used as an emergency fund. The loan may also offer a lower interest rate than some alternatives. For example, a loan on a whole life policy may offer a 5 percent interest rate, while a personal loan offers an 8 percent interest rate. The key here is to remember that taking a loan on a life insurance policy does have consequences—in the form of a reduced death benefit to your beneficiaries. Therefore, if you do take a loan, it is best to pay it back.

Quick Comparison of Insurance Types

Insurance Type	Duration	Premiums	Cash Value	Death Benefit
Term Life	Temporary	Lower for younger clients	No	Fixed (only if death occurs during the term)
Whole Life	Permanent	Level (fixed)	Yes (loan available)	Fixed
Variable Life	Permanent	Level (fixed)	Yes (invested in the market)	Can increase or decline